The Age of Broadcasting:
Radio

Edited and Introduced by
Wim Coleman and Pat Perrin

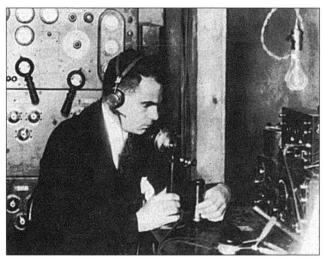

WJY, RCA's first radio studio, New Jersey, 1921 (Smithsonian)

Discovery Enterprises, Ltd.
Carlisle, Massachusetts

© Discovery Enterprises, Ltd., Carlisle, MA 1997

ISBN 1-878668-85-4 paperback edition
Library of Congress Catalog Card Number 96-86663

10 9 8 7 6 5 4 3 2 1

Printed in the United States of America

Subject Reference Guide:

The Age of Broadcasting: Radio
Edited and Introduced by Wim Coleman and Pat Perrin

Radio — U. S. History

Commercial Broadcasting — U. S. History

Radio Advertising — U. S. History

Photos/Illustrations:

Cover photo: National Museum of American History

Credits for photos and illustrations are noted in the text.

Table of Contents

Foreword 5
by Wim Coleman and Pat Perrin

Making Radio Work 8
A New Technology 9
Teaching the Spark to Talk 10

Expectations and Prophecies 13
A Radio Music Box 13
An Advertisement Attracts Attention 16
A Radio Station Opens 17
The Public Interest 18
A Smaller World 19

Who's Going to Pay for It? 20
David Sarnoff on Selling the Music Boxes 20
Private or Public Funding 21
Government Regulation 22
Advertising on the Air 23
How Do You Like That Idea? 25

You're On the Air 27
Political Broadcasting 27
A Voice Heard 'Round the World 28
Astounding Progress 29
The Merciless Medium 30
Radio Everywhere 31
Destroying Time and Space 32
Running a Radio Station 33
Broadcasting Musical Theatre 34
Sender and Receiver 35
Too Many Cooks 36

Who's in Control? 37

Teenagers Deny Mischief 37
Letters to an Editor 38
Licensing Radio 41
Radio Act of 1927 41

Who's Listening 43

Send Me a Dime 43
The Listeners Write 44
Measuring the Audience 45
Advertising for Listeners 48

Radio's Golden Age 49

The Hindenburg 50
Morrison Describes His Experience 51
Broadcasting Sports 52
Rumors of War 54
Broadcasting a War 55
From a London Rooftop 56
A Soldier Reports 57
Radio Storytelling 58
Welles on Radio Drama 61
Program Codes for Stories on the Air 63
Racial Inequality on Radio 64
A Plea for Understanding and Toleration 65
A New Code 65

Epilogue 66

Suggested Further Reading 67

About the Editors 68

Foreword

by
Wim Coleman and Pat Perrin

Today, most places in our world are linked by satellite communication, cable television, and computer networks. These potent mass technologies make it hard for us to imagine the impact broadcast radio had when it first appeared early in the twentieth century. Before radio, newspapers were the fastest and farthest-reaching forms of mass communication available. True, the telegraph could bridge huge distances. But a telegraph couldn't affect millions of people in a single instant — and radio could.

With its power to reach through the atmosphere itself, radio seemed like some sort of magic to the people who first experienced it. Of course it wasn't magic at all, but was based on the science of its day, especially the theories of Scottish physicist James Clerk Maxwell concerning electricity and electromagnetic waves. Maxwell's theories were confirmed in the late 1880s through the experiments of German physicist Heinrich Hertz. This development allowed Guglielmo Marconi to develop the wireless telegraph, which he patented in 1896. In 1901, Marconi sent the first transatlantic radio signal from England to Newfoundland. Radio soon proved important to ocean-going ships, making quick rescues possible even in poor visibility.

In 1906, Reginald Fessenden first transmitted speech. That same year, Lee De Forest invented the triode, a vacuum tube which greatly expanded the power to transmit and receive radio signals. Courtesy of this innovation, thousands of amateurs took up the hobby of radio. They started off talking back and forth to each other, then began to pick up early commercial broadcasts. During the first World War, amateur radio was banned and the Navy Department took over all broadcasting. But the ban was lifted after peace was declared, and radio grew rapidly from that time on.

The manufacturers of receivers set up broadcasting stations to support sales of their equipment. The first stations were low-powered and relatively inexpensive. Early studios were set up in unused spaces, including a former cloak closet and a ladies restroom. One person often did absolutely everything: announcing, playing music, creating sound effects, and handling the technical aspects of broadcasting. Famous people appeared for interviews, and events such as church services and sports were available for free.

But more powerful equipment became available every year, and costs rose. The one-man station expanded to include expert technicians, station managers, program directors, and others. Groups of musicians — sometimes an entire band or a small symphony orchestra — performed live on the air. These and other performers didn't appear for free anymore. Radio became a huge commercial concern, growing bigger and more influential than ever. The competition of television notwithstanding, radio remains a powerful influence on our culture to this day.

Fortunately, the history of this extraordinary medium is richly documented. This book is a compilation of some of the words, thoughts, and experiences of people who were directly involved in the beginnings and heyday of broadcast radio.

As has already been suggested, no one individual can be said to have invented radio — as Alfred N. Goldsmith and Austin C. Lescarboura said in an early history of the medium.

Source: Alfred N. Goldsmith and Austin C. Lescarboura, *This Thing Called Broadcasting: A Simple Tale of an Idea, an Experiment, a Mighty Industry, a Daily Habit, and a Basic Influence in our Modern Civilization.* New York: Henry Holt and Company, 1930, pp. v-vi.

Lee De Forest (National Archives)

To answer the question of radio paternity, one must needs know what is meant by *radio*. If we refer to the impressing of the voice on a radio wave, Reginald A. Fessenden becomes the father of radio. If conceiving the possibility of propagating music and talks to an unseen and unknown audience means radio, then Lee De Forest becomes the proud father. If by radio is meant the institutionalized syndication of programs over wire networks to scattered radio stations, then the planning mind which managed Station WEAF is the father of radio. If by radio is meant the psychological and engineering change from purely experimental radio telephony to an organized service to the interested public, then Frank Conrad of Station KDKA is the father. If the foresight to couple organized broadcasting with the quantity production of home radio sets, with all that this implies to the radio industry, be radio, then H.P. Davis, Vice-President of the Westinghouse organization is the father.

Making Radio Work

By the end of the nineteenth century, Alexander Graham Bell had made it possible to transmit sounds — including the human voice — across vast distances by means of wires. At the beginning of the twentieth century, Guglielmo Marconi made it possible to transmit telegraph signals without wires. The next step seemed obvious: to transmit voices and sounds across space without wires, just as Marconi had done for telegraph signals. Given the ingenuity of the inventors and engineers who undertook this challenge, the invention of radio was surely inevitable.

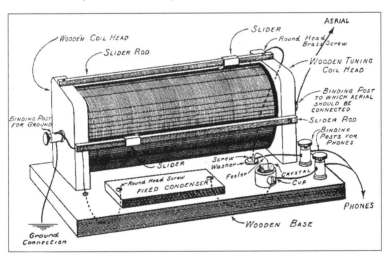

Plans for a crystal radio set. (Library of Congress)

A New Technology

Until the early twentieth century, physicists believed in "ether" — a mysterious substance which filled all space, even apparent vacuums. The existence of ether seemed like common sense. After all, didn't light waves require some sort of substance to move through? As it turned out, they did not. The concept of ether was ultimately discarded when Einstein's theories of relativity gained acceptance. But the term was still being used in early explanations of how radio worked.

Source: Frederick E. Drinker and James G. Lewis, M.E., *Radio, Miracle of the 20th Century*. Washington: National Publishing Co., in the Office of the Librarian of Congress, 1922, pp. 24-25.

Radio communication involves three definite operations: First, there must be a suitable source of radio energy, which is designated the "transmitter" capable of imparting the energy to space, or the ether, as the scientists call it. Next, the radio energy converted into vibrations of the ether, is projected through space in wave circles over the surface of the earth. The waves, naturally gradually lose their power as they extend farther and farther away from the source, just as the waves produced in a body of water by the throwing of a stone, decrease in height as the circles increase in size and the distance from the centre becomes greater. The third step is to intercept the ether waves at any desired point — to catch whatever message has been projected. For this purpose a receiving set is used.

....

...To the individual interested in the newest science the receiving set is the one big thing. To this there are five essential parts. The antenna, the lightning switch, ground connection, the actual receiving set or device, and the phone.

The received signals or waves come into the actual receiving set through the antenna and ground connection.

The antenna is therefore a highly essential factor in the big system. This is simply a wire or set of wires suspended between two highly elevated points.

If you are at all familiar with ants you will have some idea of what the antenna is. The electric experts have taken the word antenna from entomology. The wires are "sensitive feelers" which detect the waves that strike them in the air or ether space. The waves are projected from the transmission station and when they reach the antenna extending up into space they impart to it the identical wave motion.

If you lay a block of wood on the surface of a small pool near the bank or shore, and strike it sharply, it will bob up and down on the waves. A similar block of wood laid quietly on the water at the opposite side of the pool will have imparted to it the same motion when the waves created by the striking of the first block have extended across the pool. Both blocks will follow the wave undulations and move together. This is precisely what happens in radiotelephony. The antenna when struck by the ether waves moves precisely as do the waves projected from the transmission station.

Teaching the Spark to Talk

In early radio, a crystal of galena or carborundum was used to detect radio waves. These "crystal sets" could only pick up strong signals. It was the development of the electron tube that made real advancement possible. The diode tube, which detected higher-frequency waves, was invented in 1905 by Sir Ambrose Fleming. The triode was invented by Lee De Forest.

In 1899, when he was twenty-six, Lee De Forest completed a Ph.D.

program at Yale University with a dissertation on wireless telegraphy. He continued to be fascinated with broadcasting, and in 1906 he invented the triode, or Audion tube, which amplified radio signals. In 1945, Nobel Prize winner Dr. I. I. Rabi described De Forest's tube as "so outstanding in its consequences that it almost ranks with the greatest inventions of all time."

Source: Lee De Forest, Ph.D., D.S.C., "A Review of Radio," *Radio Broadcast*, Aug. 1922, p. 336.

How have we "taught the spark to talk"? As so often in the history of invention — by not doing it — by suppressing the spark!

By the little silent arc, or by the very high-frequency alternator…we first secured our sustained electrical oscillations, smooth and continuous radiations from the aerial wires.

Their frequency, as we have seen, is far beyond the range of the ear, so that although each wave gives a little kick to the distant detector, the ear listening in at the telephone hears not a sound.

But the intensity of these rapidly succeeding impulses we can vary by the voice, exactly as the voice in the ordinary telephone transmitter controls the momentary strength of the current therein flowing. We also employ the microphone, only instead of connecting it to the "line" it is inserted in the lead which runs from the oscillating system to the earth-plate.

Every inflection, every shade of articulation, the timbre of each instrument of an orchestra will be instantly carried and reproduced with surprising fidelity, notwithstanding all the strange transformations through which the original vibrations have passed.

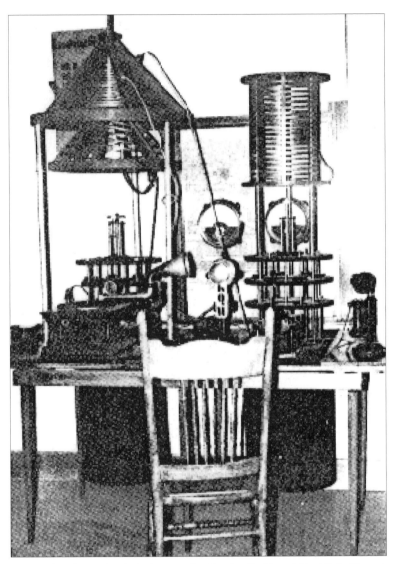

Original radio station KQW, set up by Charles D. Herrold in 1921. Now at Foothill College Electronic Museum, Los Altos, CA. Prof. Herrold started broadcasting in 1909 using modulated sparks, with his students as the audience.

Expectations and Prophecies

Once the technological problems of radio were solved, the greater challenge of defining the new medium remained. Just what was radio for, and whom could it serve? At first, it was difficult even to say just what radio was. Early on, it was called radiotelephony, and some expected it to be a means of private communication — rather like the cellular phones of today. But it soon became clear that radio was something new — a medium capable of reaching greater masses of people than anything before.

A Radio Music Box

In 1906, a fifteen-year-old Russian immigrant was hired as an office boy by The Marconi Wireless Telegraphy Company of America in New York. His name was David Sarnoff, and he was soon promoted to junior wireless operator. He was on duty on April 14, 1912, when a Morse code message arrived from the S.S. Olympic that the S.S. Titanic had run into an iceberg and was sinking. For seventy-two hours Sarnoff stayed at his set, gathering information and passing it on as the Titanic went down. Sarnoff and radio entered history along with the tragic event. In 1914, he became the contract manager of the Marconi Company. He later served as chief executive of the Radio Corporation of America (RCA) and of the National Broadcasting Corporation (NBC).

Sarnoff was a visionary who foresaw many of the uses of radio, including one which remains widespread today: the transmittal of music to a broad public.

David Sarnoff at his key at the Marconi Company's Siasconset station.

Source: A memorandum to Edward J. Nally, Vice-president and General Manager of Marconi Wireless Telegraph Company of America. Sept. 30, 1915, from David Sarnoff, *Looking Ahead: The Papers of David Sarnoff*. New York: McGraw-Hill Book Company, 1968, pp. 31-2.

I have in mind a plan of development which would make radio a "household utility" in the same sense as the piano or phonograph. The idea is to bring music into the house by wireless.

While this has been tried in the past by wires, it has been a failure because wires do not lend themselves to this scheme. With radio, however, it would seem to be entirely feasible. For example, a radiotelephone transmitter having a range of, say, 25 to 50 miles can be installed at a fixed point where instrumental or vocal music or both are produced. The problem of transmitting music has already been solved in principle, and therefore all the receivers attuned to the transmitting wavelength should be capable of receiving such music. The receiver can be designed in the form of a simple "Radio Music Box" and arranged for several different wavelengths, which should be changeable with the throwing of a single switch or pressing of a single button.

The "Radio Music Box" can be supplied with amplifying tubes and a loudspeaking telephone, all of which can be neatly mounted in one box. The box can be placed on a table in the parlor or living room, the switch set accordingly, and the transmitted music received. There should be no difficulty in receiving music perfectly when transmitted within a radius of 25 to 50 miles. Within such a radius, there reside hundreds of thousands of families; and as all can simultaneously receive from a single transmitter, there would be no question of obtaining sufficiently loud signals to make the performance enjoyable. The power of the transmitter can be made 5 kilowatts, if necessary, to cover even a short radius of 25 to 50 miles, thereby giving extra-loud signals in the home if desired. The use of head telephones would be obviated by this method. The development of a small loop antenna to go with each "Radio Music Box" would likewise solve the antenna problem.

The same principle can be extended to numerous other fields—as, for example, receiving lectures at home which can be made perfectly audible; also, events of national importance can be simultaneously announced and received. Baseball scores can be transmitted in the air or by the use of one set installed at the Polo Grounds. The same would be true of other cities. By the purchase of a "Radio Music Box," they could enjoy concerts, lectures, music, recitals, etc., which might be going on in the nearest city within their radius. While I have indicated a few of the most probable fields of usefulness for such a device, there are numerous other fields to which the principle can be extended....

An Advertisement Attracts Attention

In 1920, Dr. Frank Conrad was assistant chief engineer at Westinghouse Electric and Manufacturing Company of Pittsburgh, Pennsylvania. A ham radio operator, Conrad had earlier set up an experimental radio station, 8XK, in his own garage. Conrad gave talks over the radio and played recorded music. He even announced a schedule of "broadcasts," which was the first use of that term. When Conrad's personal record supply ran out, he was offered records by a local music store (if he would mention their name, which he did). Interest in the broadcasts grew so strong that a Pittsburgh department store, the Joseph Horne Company, ran an ad for wireless sets in the Pittsburgh Sun on September 29, 1920.

Source: Irving Settel, *A Pictorial History of Radio*, New York: Grosset & Dunlap, 1960, 1967, p. 36.

Air Concert
"Picked Up"
By Radio Here

Victrola music, played into the air over a wireless telephone, was "picked up" by listeners on the wireless receiving station which was recently installed here for patrons interested in wireless experiments. The Concert was heard Thursday night about 10 o'clock and continued about 20 minutes. Two orchestra numbers, a soprano solo-which rang particularly high and clear-and a juvenile "talking piece" constituted the program.

The music was from a Victrola pulled up close to the transmitter of a wireless telephone in the home of Frank Conrad, Penn and Peebles avenues, Wilkinsburg. Mr. Conrad is a wireless enthusiast and "puts on" the wireless concerts periodically for the entertainment of the many people in this district who have wireless sets.

Amateur Wireless Sets, made by the maker of the Set which is in operation in our store, are on sale here, $10.00 up.

A Radio Station Opens

The Joseph Horne Company advertisement was seen by Harry P. Davis,
Vice-President of the Westinghouse Electric and Manufacturing Company.
Seven years later, in an address at the Graduate School of Business Adminis-
tration of Harvard University, Davis spoke about the decision made in 1920
for Westinghouse to build a radio station. On November 2, 1920, Westinghouse
opened station KDKA, directed by Dr. Frank Conrad. For a time, KDKA
operated out of a tent on the roof of a Westinghouse plant.

Source: Archer, Gleason L., LL.D., *History of Radio to 1926*, New York, The American
Historical Society, Inc., 1938, pp. 200-201.

An advertisement of a local department store in a Pittsburgh newspaper, calling attention to a stock of radio receivers which could be used to receive the programs...
caused the thought to come to me that the efforts that
were then being made to develop radio telephony as a
confidential means of communication were wrong, and
that instead its field was really one of wide publicity, in
fact, the only means of instantaneous collective communication ever devised. Right in our grasp, therefore, we
had that service which we had been thinking about and
endeavoring to formulate.

Here was an idea of limitless opportunity if it could be
"put across." A little study of this thought developed great
possibilities. It was felt that there was something that
would make a new public service of a kind certain to create
epochal changes in the then accepted everyday affairs,
quite as vital as had been the introduction of the telephone
and telegraph, or the application of electricity to lighting
and to power. We became convinced that we had in our
hands in this idea the instrument that would prove to be
the greatest and most direct means of mass communication and mass education that had ever appeared.

The Public Interest

The new medium caught the attention of Secretary of Commerce Herbert Hoover, who addressed his newly-appointed Radio Commission at a 1922 conference in Washington, D.C.

Source: Frederick E. Drinker and James G. Lewis, M.E., *op. cit.*, p. 174.

We are indeed today upon the threshold of a new means of widespread communication of intelligence that has the most profound importance from the point of view of public education and public welfare....

I think that it will be agreed at the outset that the use of the radiotelephone for communication between single individuals as in the case of the ordinary telephone is a perfectly hopeless notion. Obviously if ten million telephone subscribers are crying through the air for their mates they will never make a junction; the ether will be filled with frantic chaos, with no communication of any kind possible. In other words, the wireless telephone has one definite field, and that is for spread of certain predetermined material of public interest from central stations. This material must be limited to news, to education, to entertainment, and the communication of such commercial matters as are of importance to large groups of the community at the same time.

It is therefore primarily a question of broadcasting, and it becomes of primary public interest to say who is to do the broadcasting, under what circumstances, and with what type of material. It is inconceivable that we should allow so great a possibility for service, for news, for entertainment, for education, and for vital commercial purposes, to be drowned in advertising chatter, or for commercial purposes that can be quite well served by our other means of communication.

A Smaller World

It soon became apparent that the most powerful form of mass communication ever imagined had arrived. In 1922, Frederick E. Drinker and James G. Lewis made this euphoric assessment of the new medium in their book Radio: Miracle of the 20th Century.

Source: Drinker and Lewis, *op. cit.*, p. 32.

Measured in units of time the world is now about one-tenth of a second wide. Radio is the new instrument with which we measure the world's width in this astonishing fashion. Viewed through this magic reducing glass created by man the earth, for all its eight thousand miles diameter, seems to have shriveled into a ball so small that it might be held in the hand of a playful child.

San Francisco no longer is three thousand miles distant from New York. It is within speaking distance. The whole world has become one vast auditorium in which the speech of one man may be heard by all.

Who's Going to Pay for It?

How was radio broadcasting to be paid for? Broadcasts obviously couldn't be sold like newspapers or magazines, and listeners didn't need tickets — they only needed a receiving set. The magazine Radio Broadcast *even offered a prize of $500 for "the Most Practicable and Workable Solution of a Difficult Problem." The winner, H. D. Kellogg, Jr., proposed a tax of $2 on each tube and $.50 on each crystal used in a receiver, with the tax to be administered by a Federal Bureau of Broadcasting. (Source:* Radio Broadcast, *March, 1925, pp. 863-864.) Other ideas were bandied about — some of them workable, some of them not.*

David Sarnoff on Selling the Music Boxes

When he proposed the "Radio Music Box" in 1915, David Sarnoff also suggested that the sales of radios and transmitters could pay for broadcasting. Note that Sarnoff's only mention of advertising is that which the product would bring to itself.

Source: *Looking Ahead: The Papers of David Sarnoff.* New York: McGraw-Hill Book Company, 1968, pp. 31-2.

The manufacture of the "Radio Music Box," including antenna, in large quantities would make possible their sale at a moderate figure of perhaps $75 per outfit. The main revenue to be derived would be from the sale of "Radio Music Boxes," which, if manufactured in quantities of a hundred thousand or so, could yield a handsome profit when sold at the price mentioned above. Secondary sources of revenue would be from the sale of transmitters....

Aside from the profit to be derived from this proposition, the possibilities for advertising for the company are tremendous, for its name would ultimately be brought into the household, and wireless would receive national and universal attention.

Private or Public Funding

The idea of financing broadcasts purely through sales of radios and transmitters was, of course, unrealistic. Other solutions were proposed in the pages of the magazine Radio Broadcast. *The following editorial suggested that radio be financed by public funds as a public good — much like schools, highways, and libraries.*

Source: "Radio Currents: An Editorial Interpretation," *Radio Broadcast*, May 1922, pp. 3-4.

[A] powerful station could be put up and operated at a cost less than that required for a reasonable sized library, and there is no doubt that a properly conducted radio broadcasting station can do at least as great an educational work as does the average library. This is not said to disparage the endowment of libraries but to point out another way for the wealthy citizen to invest part of his excess wealth for the public good....

Another possible scheme for the maintenance of suitable broadcasting stations is by contributions to a common fund, which would be controlled by an elected board; this would be one of the most difficult ways of carrying on the work, for the reason that any one can listen in on a broadcasting station whether he contributes to its support or not....

A third way, and probably the most reasonable way, to operate the transmitting station is by municipal financing. A weird scheme this will undoubtedly appear to many, but upon analysis it will be found not so strange, even to those who have no socialistic tendencies. In New York City, for example, large sums of money are spent annually in maintaining free public lectures, given on various topics of interest; the attendance at one of these lectures may average two or three hundred people. The same lecture delivered from a broadcasting station would be heard by several thousand people....The cost of such a project would probably be less than that for the scheme at present used and the number of people who would benefit might be immeasurably greater.

Governmental Regulation

H. M. Taylor, a contributor to Radio Broadcast, *made an even stronger argument for government intervention in the new medium. Here is an early hint of public broadcasting. Perhaps, Taylor also suggested, radio should be thought of as a utility.*

Source: H. M. Taylor, "Random Observation on Running a Broadcasting Station," *Radio Broadcast*, July 1922, p. 226.

[S]ome new method must be devised for financing radio broadcasting. Obviously, it is an enormous expense to the operating companies for which they are compensated by the sale of receiving equipment. But other companies can sell receiving equipment which will receive broadcasting programmes as well as those operating broadcasting stations. Far be it from me to mean by this statement that the sale of radio equipment should be limited to those at present operating broadcasting stations, but on the other hand the extra broadcasting expense, which benefits everyone in the business, cannot in fairness to all be borne by a few. Why can't there be a national broadcasting association, under government supervision, to the support of which every manufacturer of radio receiving equipment of a certain capitalization contributes? This is one suggestion. Another is that the government conduct and control broadcasting as it does the mails, or as cities do the water supply. These are merely suggestions and of course only a few of many possible ones. That radio broadcasting in some form will continue and improve and become more widespread is, to those close to this new, epochal industry, as certain as sunrise.

Advertising on the Air

On-the-air advertising began very early in the history of broadcast radio. Station WEAF was established in 1922 by AT&T for the purpose of selling commercial radio time. The first commercial was read on Monday, August 28, 1922, from 5:15 - 5:30 p.m.

Source: Archer, Gleason L., LL.D., *op. cit.,* pp. 397-9.

BROADCASTING PROGRAM
HAWTHORNE COURT INTRODUCTION
This afternoon the radio audience is to be addressed by Mr. Blackwell of the Queensboro Corporation, who through arrangements made by the Griffin Radio Service, Inc., will say a few words concerning Nathaniel Hawthorne and the desirability of fostering the helpful community spirit and the healthful, unconfined home life that were Hawthorne ideals. Ladies and Gentlemen: Mr. Blackwell.

It is fifty-eight years since Nathaniel Hawthorne, the greatest of American fictionists, passed away. To honor his memory the Queensboro Corporation, creator and operator of the tenant-owned system of apartment homes at Jackson Heights, New York City, has named its latest group of high-grade dwellings "Hawthorne Court."

I wish to thank those within sound of my voice for the broadcasting opportunity afforded me to urge this vast radio audience to seek the recreation and the daily comfort of the home removed from the congested part of the city, right at the boundaries of God's great outdoors, and within a few minutes by subway from the business section of Manhattan. This sort of residential environment strongly influenced Hawthorne, America's greatest writer of fiction....

....

Thousands of dwellers in the congested district apartments want to remove to healthier and happier sections but they don't know and they can't seem to get into the belief that their living situation and home environment can be improved. Many of them balk at buying a house in the country or the suburbs and becoming a commuter. They have visions of toiling down in a cellar with a sullen furnace, or shovelling snow, or of blistering palms pushing a clanking lawn mower. They can't seem to overcome the pessimistic inertia that keeps pounding into their brains that their crowded, unhealthy, unhappy living conditions cannot be improved.

....

...Imagine an apartment to live in at a place where you and your neighbor join the same community clubs, organizations and activities, where you golf with your neighbor, tennis with your neighbor, bowl with your neighbor and join him in a long list of outdoor and indoor pleasure-giving health-giving activities.

....

Right at your door is such an opportunity. It only requires the will to take advantage of it all. You owe it to yourself and you owe it to your family to leave the hemmed-in, sombre-hued, artificial apartment life of the congested city section and enjoy what nature intended you should enjoy....

...Let me close by urging that you hurry to the apartment home near the green fields and the neighborly atmosphere right on the subway without the expense and the trouble of a commuter, where health and community happiness beckon — the community life and friendly environment that Hawthorne advocated.

How Do You Like That Idea?

Not surprisingly, some people quickly became as disenchanted with broad-cast advertising as many of us are today. This dissatisfaction was expressed in the pages of Radio Broadcast.

Source: Joseph H. Jackson, "Should Radio Be Used for Advertising?" *Radio Broadcast,* November, 1922 p. 72.

"Advertising by Radio" is his new name; and a very trouble-some pest he is likely to become unless something is done, and that quickly.

No one who reads this article will have to consider very long what broadcasting advertising implies, before the presence of the difficulty becomes apparent enough. The very thought of such a thing growing to be common practice is sufficient to give any true radio enthusiast the cold shakes. And he doesn't need to be a dyed-in-the-shellac radio man to see the point, either; the veriest tyro with his brand-new crystal set can realize, if he has listened in only once, what it would mean to have the air filled with advertising matter in and out of season; to have his ears bombarded with advertisers' eulogies every time he dons a pair of head phones....

Supposing — just supposing — you are sitting down, head phones clamped to your ears, or loud-speaker distorting a trifle less than usual, enjoying a really excellent radio concert. A famous soprano has just sung your favorite song, and you're drawing a deep breath, sorry that it's over. Your thoughts, carried back to some pleasant memory by the magic of the radio, are still full of the melody. You are feeling sort of soothed and good-natured and at peace with the world. All of a sudden a gruff voice or a whining voice or a nasal voice or some other kind of a voice says "Good Morning! Have you used Hare's Soap?" Or maybe a sweet, girlish baritone implores you "Ask for Never-Hole Sox. There's a Reason. You just *know* she wears 'em."

Well, how about it. Do you like the idea? Can you picture to yourself the horror of sitting down to listen to a good song or two, or perhaps a newsy chat on the events of the day, and then being forced to listen to a broadcasting programme that is nine tenths advertising matter?

You're On the Air

Radio became an increasingly important part of American life during the 1920s. Music and story readings were soon joined by sports, education, religion, farm news, and other programs. In 1921, the Dempsey-Carpentier boxing match was broadcast with borrowed and patched-together equipment to 200,000 people. Over the next few years, additional boxing matches, baseball games, and boat races were announced over the air. News and politics quickly found their way into broadcast radio. The new form of mass communication generated a lot of excitement — as well as more than a few concerns.

Political Broadcasting

Radio broadcasting entered the political sphere the very moment it was born, with KDKA's reporting of the 1920 presidential election. In their early history of radio, Alfred N. Goldsmith and Austin C. Lescarboura documented the incredible rise in political reporting on radio.

Source: Alfred N. Goldsmith and Austin C. Lescarboura, *op. cit.*, p. 205.

Looking over the presidential elections since the dawn of radio we find that in 1916 Dr. Lee De Forest broadcast the returns of the Wilson-Hughes election from his High Bridge station to perhaps a dozen people with receiving sets. In 1920 KDKA opened with the returns of the Harding-Cox battle. About 50 people heard the returns on sets manufactured specially for the occasion. In 1924 the Coolidge-Davis returns were heard by about 20,000,000, and four years later the Hoover-Smith election returns came over the air to about 50,000,000.

A Voice Heard 'Round the World

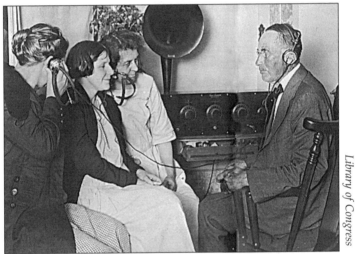

Library of Congress

Calvin Coolidge's son John and friends in Plymouth, VT listen to the President telling the nation he will run for office. (August 14, 1924)

In 1921, President Warren G. Harding's Armistice Day speech was the first commercial radio broadcast of an address by a chief executive. A New York Times *editorial commented on this groundbreaking event.*

Source: *New York Times*, November 1, 1921. In J. Fred MacDonald, *Don't Touch that Dial! Radio Programming in American Life, 1920-1960*, Chicago: Nelson-Hall, 1979, p. 7.

When the very voice of the President of the Republic can be heard by tens of thousands of people, in hall and park and street, at the selfsame moment in New York and San Francisco, and when a wireless message from the President can be heard almost in the same instant, as it was a few days earlier by the heads of twenty-eight different Governments before it returned, within the space of seven seconds, from its circuit of the earth, one's imagination leaps to the political, social and moral consequences of these physical achievements.

Astounding Progress

Such developments were not lost on politicians themselves. In 1922, a conference was held at the Department of Commerce in Washington by members of the Radio Commission appointed by Secretary Hoover. Hoover opened the conference with a comment on the progress of the new medium.

Source: Gleason L. Archer, LL.D., *op.cit.*, p. 248.

We have witnessed in the last four or five months one of the most astounding things that has come under my observation of American life. This Department estimates that today more than 600,000 (one estimate being 1,000,000) persons possess wireless telephone receiving sets, whereas there were less than fifty thousand such sets a year ago. We are indeed today upon the threshold of a new means of widespread communication of intelligence that has the most profound importance from the point of view of public education and public welfare.

The Merciless Medium

What kind of influence was mass broadcasting to have on American political life? Early commentators assumed that it would be extremely beneficial. After all, democracy depended upon an informed public, and radio had the power to spread information like no other medium ever had. More than that, radio seemed to have the power to cut through hocum and nonsense, as this Saturday Evening Post *editorial contended.*

Source: An editorial, "The Spellbinder and the Radio," *The Saturday Evening Post*, August 23, 1924 (no page # given). (Found in Alfred N. Goldsmith and Austin C. Lescarboura, *op. cit.*, p. 198.

The Democratic Convention was held in New York, but all America attended it....The convention ...emphasized what is to become the main function and the greatest service of the radio. It gives events of national importance a national audience. Incidentally, also it uncovered another benefit radio seems destined to bestow upon us, the debunking of present-day oratory and the setting up of higher standards in public speaking....Orators up to the present have been getting by on purely adventitious aids. A good personality, a musical voice, a power of dramatic gesture have served to cover up baldness of thought and limping phraseology....The radio is even more merciless than the printed report as a conveyor of oratory....It is uncompromising and literal transmission. The listeners follow the speech with one sense only. There is nothing to distract their attention....Radio constitutes the severest test for speakers of the rough-and-ready, catch-as-catch-can school, and reputations are going to shrink badly now that the whole nation is listening in. Silver-tongued orators whose fame has been won before sympathetic audiences are going to scale down to their real stature when the verdict comes from radio audiences.

Radio Everywhere

Perhaps most impressively, radio seemed able to inform and educate those who had little access to schooling or even an ordinary church service. In an article for Radio Broadcast, *contributor Sue M. Harrison extolled the power of radio to reach those at the margins of society.*

Source: Sue M. Harrison, "Radio in Remote Regions: A Sign in the Wilderness," *Radio Broadcast*, Oct. 1922, p. 524.

I had been visiting in Ashville, North Carolina for about a week, when my hostess suggested a trip through the mountains for the coming Sunday. About four o'clock in the afternoon we passed a little school house, deserted as far as school teaching was concerned, but far from deserted as we saw it. About sixty mountaineers were studying this sign on the front of the building:

Preaching Here Tonite By Radiophone
Mountaineers All Welcome Free

Radiophone — the latest and most wonderful product of science — here in a desolate place where there had been no school for years, where even the telephone was a mysterious thing — often unknown.

Destroying Time and Space

The beneficial possibilities of radio often generated dazzling praise —
particularly from those in the radio business. Here are some comments from
Owen D. Young, Chairman of the Board of RCA, speaking at the opening
ceremony for stations WJZ and WJY in 1923.

Source: Owen D. Young's speech, as quoted in *Radio Broadcast*, July, 1923, p. 255. (From Archer, *op. cit.*, p. 304.)

Broadcasting has appealed to the imagination as no other scientific development of the time. Its ultimate effect upon the educational, social, political, and religious life of our country and of the world is quite beyond our ability to prophesy.

Already it is bringing to the farmer, market, weather, and crop reports as well as time signals, which cannot help but be of an economic value. In remote communities, where the country parson is no longer in attendance at Sunday morning services, it is filling a great need in spiritual life. Its educational possibilities are being investigated by our foremost national and state educators. It is taking entertainment from the large centers to individual homes. To the blind and the sick it has unfolded a new and richer life. For the purpose of communication it has destroyed time and space.

Running a Radio Station

Of course, one of the most exciting aspects of early radio was the opportunity to innovate in a new medium. In the early 1920s, few of the rules and techniques of broadcast radio had been set in stone. The possibilities were intoxicating—and also a bit daunting, as H. M. Taylor observed in the pages of Radio Broadcast.

Source: H. M. Taylor, "Random Observation on Running a Broadcasting Station: Success Demands a New Type of Impresario Who is a Sort of Combination Editor and Theatrical Manager," *Radio Broadcast*, July 1922, p. 223.

Running a broadcasting station is a novel, not to say fascinating experience. There is no precedent to follow. There is no literature on the subject (that is, no literature in the usual sense; I do not refer to letters from the radio audience advising how the broadcasting station should be run). Each broadcaster, generally speaking, has to work out his own code of rules, use his own common sense, make his own formulae, and profit by his own mistakes. Without doubt a broadcasting technique will soon be worked out. It is being done now—rapidly. But in the present state of the radio art, this technique is incomplete — embryonic.

There are two major problems to be encountered by those running a broadcasting station. One is the mechanical or technical side. The other, for want of a more descriptive characterization, may be termed the human side. Both are of the utmost importance. The public, which is the ultimate judge of the success of a broadcasting station, can never be satisfied if one side is defective. Good programmes count for nothing if the technical mechanism does not put them out so that the average person can receive them clearly and fairly easily. And perfect reproduction and transmission of programmes avails little if the operator in charge does not possess a pleasing voice, speak correctly, put on his numbers without long waits and possess a certain indescribable mental agility of his own. Then the artists who entertain play an important part, of course, in the success or failure of the broadcast. To find an operator who understands human nature so that he can be sympathetic and at the same time manage temperamental artists, successful business men and others who have attained prominence in world affairs, who can surmount the internal friction ever present in all organizations, and who, in addition, thoroughly comprehends the scientific and mechanical operation of the broadcasting equipment, is difficult, to say the least. As the old farmer at the circus said, "there ain't no such animile."

Broadcasting Musical Theatre

The business of pure entertainment was particularly adventurous in radio's early days. Bertha Brainard, on the staff of WJY and WJZ, arranged and introduced the first play to be broadcast, followed by many more. She wrote an account of her experiences for the authors of Broadcasting: Its New Day.

Source: Samuel L. Rothafel and Raymond Francis Yates, *Broadcasting: Its New Day*, New York: The Century Co., 1925, pp. 59-62.

WJZ of the Radio Corporation of America was the first radio station to broadcast a theatrical production directly from the stage. As long ago as 1922 a Broadway play was given to all parts of the country via the air....

...A year or so ago, we broadcasted dramatic productions, but the wishes of our listeners-in and the advice of our technical department have convinced us that musical plays only are what we should broadcast....

....

The location of the microphones is carefully studied. ...Not so long ago we did place a microphone on a mantel in front of which a long scene was played, and on which a real clock was busily ticking. This ticking could be heard throughout the broadcasting of this scene. The next morning our mail brought a complaint from an irate listener that our carrier wave was noisy. He could hear it clicking regularly during most of the play.

Sender and Receiver

More skeptical commentators took early note that broadcast radio had built-in limitations despite its many strengths. It was hardly what we would today call an "interactive" medium. The role of the listener was inevitably passive — and even a bit helpless, as was observed in this Radio Broadcast *commentary.*

Source: "Radio Currents: An Editorial Interpretation," *Radio Broadcast*, May 1922, p. 2.

In this latest application of scientific achievement there are two essential parts, a transmitting station from which the radio broadcasting is done and the station at which it is received. If you have a receiving station, you come under our classification of *receiver*, and it is in your attitude toward the transmitting station that we are interested. Did it ever occur to you how very helpless you are in this new activity? You turn on your switches and wait — if you hear nothing you conclude the transmitting station has not started so you wait and wonder what is going to be sent out when it does start. It may be a selection from "Aida", wonderfully executed, or it may be nothing but a scratchy, cracked, phonograph record. You have nothing to say about it, you pay nothing for it, and, still more to the point, you have no rights in the matter at all. You are not alone in this game of watching and waiting — there are hundreds of thousands of others, and soon there will be millions of people doing the same thing.

The rate of increase in the number of people who spend at least a part of their evening in listening in is almost incomprehensible. To those who have recently tried to purchase receiving equipment, some idea of this increase has undoubtedly occurred, as they stood perhaps in the fourth or fifth row at the radio counter waiting their turn only to be told when they finally reached the counter that they might place an order and it would be filled when possible.

Too Many Cooks?

Ironically, perhaps the greatest difficulty faced by broadcast radio in its infancy arose directly out of its own sudden and spectacular growth. This Radio Broadcast *editorial focused on the especially troublesome issue of licensing in a medium seemingly run amok.*

Source: An editorial, "The March of Radio: Too Many Cooks are Spoiling our Broth," *Radio Broadcast*, November 1922, p. 3.

Every month sees a remarkable growth in the number of stations licensed for radio broadcasting. This might be taken as a sign of the healthy growth of the new art, but a little reflection seems to point to the opposite conclusion. Apparently, a broadcasting license is to be had for the asking. The question now arises: Is this encouragement of broadcasting stations the policy which will make for the best development of radio and its appreciation by the listening public? It seems to us that a curb should be put upon the licensing of broadcasting stations or there will soon be country-wide troubles of the kind which recently occurred near New York — conflicts between the various stations for the most desirable hours and the resulting interference of signals between the several stations, which made listening-in no pleasure.

There are at present nearly 500 licensed broadcasting stations in the United States, and this list is being augmented each week; in one week recently there were 26 new licenses issued. Probably the majority of these stations are being operated by manufacturers and dealers, but many are controlled by the press. It looks as if we shall soon have 1000 licensed stations, which means that it is about time to inquire how many of them will be operated in such a fashion as to increase the interest of the public in radio and how many of them will merely send out advertising noise.

Who's in Control?

One of today's great controversies concerns freedom of speech on the Internet. We may even find ourselves imagining that computer networks present unprecedented problems regarding censorship vs. First Amendment rights. In fact, this is far from true. In its early days, radio broadcasting posed similar dilemmas. Nobody had ever experienced a medium with such power to inform — or to annoy. Indeed, almost as soon as Morse-code messages began to be exchanged by wireless, some people were offended by some communications. But how could objectionable material be kept off the air in a free republic? It is a question, of course, which still haunts us today.

Teenagers Deny Mischief

Today, we call them "hackers" or "crackers": technological prodigies — some of them children — who wreak havoc in the world of mass communications. Although they weren't called hackers or crackers then, young pranksters plagued early wireless pathways. They found it especially easy to misrepresent themselves, since no one could trace a broadcast back to its source. This 1910 article from the New York Times *relates a typical problem.*

Source: "Deny Wireless Mischief: Young Experimenters Say They Have Not Power to Reach Distant Stations," *The New York Times*, January 30, 1910, p. 4.

MONTCLAIR, N.J., Jan. 29. — On behalf of the amateur wireless operators of Montclair, some 140 in number, who have been accused of sending profane and indecent messages through the air, Arthur P. Morgand and A. G. Cole, two boys who have been pioneers in the local experiments, have come to the defense of their colleagues in a public statement. They deny that the wireless amateurs in Montclair have offended by sending out indecent messages or causing trouble by sending false information to Government stations by use of "stolen codes."

They assert that there is no wireless station in this town which can transmit as far as Newport, R.I., whither, it was charged, the profane messages were sent, or over a radius of more than fifteen miles, and this only under exceptional weather conditions, while there are not more than six of the stations that can transmit more than two miles. The boys say they never use "stolen codes" to give false or other orders to the Government stations.

The local wireless amateurs assert that the persons who are agitating Government supervision of wireless are the representatives of a commercial concern which wishes to gain and hold a monopoly of the air for its own business to the exclusion of all competitors and the experimenters, and which is at present using petty interference troubles as a means to this end.

Letters to an Editor

With the advent of radio broadcasting, the threat of prankster outsiders waned; they couldn't compete with the powerful signals put out by commercial stations. Then a new question arose: What should commercial stations be allowed to broadcast? As it did so often with troubling issues in the new medium, the magazine Radio Broadcast *invited comments on this question.*

Source: "What Our Readers Write Us," in *Radio Broadcast*, Aug. 1924, p. 432.

A great tempest in a newspaper occurred in New York recently when WHN lent itself to broadcast an appeal by a certain theatrical producer for "fresh" chorus girls who aspired to life under the permanent wave. There were those who thought, and delayed not in expressing themselves, that to use radio thus in invading homes with an appeal of that sort was nothing short of criminal. And there were those who did not take the matter very seriously, and trusted to the judgment and balance of the girls and their mothers. The two letters below discuss both sides of the subject.

Editor, Radio Broadcast,
Doubleday, Page & Co.,
Garden City, L.I.

Dear Sir.

The First Amendment to the Constitution prohibits Congress from "abridging the freedom of speech," and surely this includes broadcasting. Even when advertising is broadcast it should not be censored, unless we are to censor advertisements in the Sunday papers and in weekly periodicals.

Yet scores of mothers have appealed to prohibit a broadcasting station in New York City from announcing that a theatrical producer will give tryouts to girls who aspire to be actresses. Do the mothers actually think that their daughters will be tempted by the unseen spokesman of the devil and will depart the home in order to earn their own living? If the opportunity of thus giving pleasure to countless multitudes appeals to the daughters, surely the mothers, who brought them up, have only themselves to blame.

G.N.B., Montclair, New Jersey

Editor, Radio Broadcast,
Doubleday, Page & Co.,
Garden City, L.I.

Dear Sir.

Twice a day, during the morning and in the middle of the evening, an appeal has been broadcast from a New York station for girls with "good figures, pretty faces, and neat ankles" to appear arrayed in bathing suits on a theater roof where they are to be photographed as entries in a contest, in which 116 will be chosen as members of a chorus for a Broadway musical comedy. It is said that several hundred respond to the invitation every day.

There is no doubt about the legal right of a broadcasting station to lend itself to such a scheme. But this is a question of morality and of good taste, not of law. The greatest blessing of radio is at the same time a great danger, and surely such an appeal to the public, in the privacy of their homes, suggests that society approves of the life of the chorus girl. The bad influence which results from this will appear in children's thoughts if not in their actions. It is surely another case of misplaced emphasis, by which the younger generation decides that the chorus girl (as previously it had decided that the movie actress) is a more admirable member of society than is the social worker or the missionary. We have had enough publicity for the acting profession, with the sordid details of their life, without this, the latest and most degraded form of it.

B.R.D., Cold Spring Harbor, New York.

Licensing Radio

In 1912, the first radio licensing law was passed by Congress and signed by President Taft. The act required station and operator licenses, and allowed the Secretary of Commerce and Labor to assign wave lengths and time limits. It gave priority to distress signals and provided penalties for fraudulent transmissions.

During the 1920s, censorship became an issue in many areas of American life. State boards censored movies and stage plays. In 1925 a state law forbidding the teaching of evolution was brought to court in the Scopes trial. Afterwards, the 69th Congress entertained — and voted down — a proposed amendment to ban discussions of evolution on radio. There was much discussion during this period about the definitions of terms such as indecency and obscenity.

Among the questions addressed by the Radio Act of 1927 were: "equal time" for political broadcasts; advertising and promotion; freedom of speech; and obscenity.

Radio Act of 1927

Source: Eric Barnouw, *A Tower in Babel: A History of Broadcasting in the United States*, Volume 1-to 1933, New York: Oxford University, 1966. The following is from the complete text of the Radio Act of 1927, Appendix B, pp. 309-10 and 312.

SEC. 18: If any licensee shall permit any person who is a legally qualified candidate for any public office to use a broadcasting station, he shall afford equal opportunities to all other such candidates for that office in the use of such broadcasting station, and the licensing authority shall make rules and regulations to carry this provision into effect: *Provided*, That such licensee shall have no power of censorship over the material broadcast under the provisions of this paragraph. No obligation is hereby imposed upon any licensee to allow the use of its station by any such candidate.

SEC. 19: All matter broadcast by any radio station for which service, money, or any other valuable consideration is directly or indirectly paid, or promised to or charged or accepted by, the station so broadcasting, from any person, firm, company, or corporation, shall, at the time the same is so broadcast, be announced as paid for or furnished, as the case may be, by such person, firm, company, or corporation.

SEC. 29. Nothing in this Act shall be understood or construed to give the licensing authority the power of censorship over the radio communications or signals transmitted by any radio station, and no regulation or condition shall be promulgated or fixed by the licensing authority which shall interfere with the right of free speech by means of radio communication. No person within the jurisdiction of the United States shall utter any obscene, indecent, or profane language by means of radio communication.

Who's Listening?

Broadcast radio was an eerie medium to its first participants — particularly announcers and performers. A person stood alone in a room in front of a microphone and spoke, read, or sang — but to whom? On stage, a performer felt the presence of live audience members, saw their faces, heard their laughter and applause, sensed their excitement or their boredom. This was not so in a radio studio. How could one know if thousands of people were listening — or no one at all?

This question was more than just a matter of performers' vanity. Since radio was a commercial medium, broadcasters simply had to find out how many people were listening — and who these people were.

Send Me a Dime

Performers accustomed to the presence of a live audience found radio especially unnerving. This little story about Eddie Cantor, who learned his craft in vaudeville, burlesque, and on Broadway, is a case in point.

Source: *New York Sun*, March 3, 1934 (In Archer, *op. cit.*, p. 220).

An interesting anecdote has been handed down of Eddie Cantor's introduction to radio. It occurred at Station WDY. The banjo-eyed comedian was nervous when he approached the microphone. Then when his best jokes evoked no ripples of mirth Cantor fell into a sort of panic. He continued to the end of the program, however, but before leaving the microphone expressed his doubt that anyone had actually heard his broadcast. Then he flung the challenge into the ether for anyone who had heard him to send him a dime to be donated to some charity. The shower of dimes that came to him through the mail convinced the doubting Cantor that radio broadcasting actually had an extensive listening public.

The Listeners Write

Of course, broadcasters did get regular feedback from audience members in the form of correspondence — although it offered little quantitative data regarding the size and makeup of radio audiences. Some of this feedback was helpful, while some of it was bizarre, as is suggested by this 1922 commentary in the magazine Radio Broadcast.

Source: H. M. Taylor, "Random Observation on Running a Broadcasting Station" *Radio Broadcast*, July 1922, p. 226.

A woman writes that her husband is a night watchman and does not wake up until 5 o'clock in the afternoon. He has a half hour to listen in at that time and two hours when he comes home in the morning between 8 and 10 o'clock. Couldn't we broadcast then? Dealers and merchants want broadcasting between 12 and one o'clock so that people can listen in on their noon hour, (a good idea). A young man wanted broadcasting after 11 P.M. because he didn't get home until that hour, as he attended night school three nights a week and worked evenings the rest of the time....A woman who signed her name and address wrote in and said — "We enjoy your performance very much each evening and always have six or seven people listening. To keep husbands home at night 'Get a Radio,' says I. Be it said, friend husband even comes home in the middle of the afternoon now to hear your broadcasting."

Sometimes people make really alarming requests and are greatly incensed when we are unable to comply. A woman in New England wrote in recently that she wanted us to broadcast some dance music on Friday. "It must be next Friday," she said, "because I have got to be out both Wednesday and Thursday evenings." As my secretary says, "You'd almost think they were paying for it."

Measuring the Audience

Unsolicited reactions were hardly enough to satisfy advertisers when they began paying for air time. It became very important to know how many people were listening and who they were. Radio stations began to encourage mail responses through free offers, contests, or simply by asking listeners to write in. Some broadcasters also encouraged phone-in responses by playing specific musical numbers on request. Offers of free items also brought in many phone calls. In 1932, the offer of a free angel food cake to the first ten callers to a Minneapolis station completely tied up the phone system with 7000 calls. (Source: *Broadcast Advertising*, V, September, 1932, p. 28.)

Telephone surveys were developed to find out more about the makeup of audiences, and a number of different companies sprang up to take over that job for the stations. One of the earliest was the Cooperative Analysis of Broadcasting, or CAB, inaugurated by the Association of National Advertisers in March, 1930. It furnished various reports to advertisers and agencies. These were based on telephone interviews in which people were asked what they had listened to on their radios during a particular period. CAB covered thirty-three large cities, completing 21,000 calls per week, and based their ratings on a two-week period. (Source: H. M. Beville, Jr., Research Manager, National Broadcasting Co., *Social Stratification of the Radio Audience: A Study Made for The Princeton Radio Research Project*, 1939, 1940, pp. 3-6.)

Another firm, C. E. Hooper, Inc., also furnished reports to advertisers, agencies, and broadcasters. This firm's technique was "coincidental telephone interviewing," meaning that respondents were interviewed while a program was actually on the air. (Source: Beville, *op. cit.,* pp. 8-13.)

The conclusions these firms reached were sometimes surprising and hard to explain. For example, researcher H. M. Beville here discusses different listening habits of high income and low income audiences.

Source: Beville, *op. cit.,* pages v-vi.

When the audience of a serious musical program is analyzed, good music is shown to be the monopoly of the upper income classes. The audience decreases markedly with decreasing income. This might have been expected, but it is important to see it documented as clearly as it is in these data. On the other hand, it will be seen that when the audience to a dramatic program is analyzed, it shows a sharp increase of listening in the lower income groups, a result not so simple to anticipate. Even some of the "highbrow" dramatic programs show this trend, which leads to the very interesting question as to why the interest in dramatizations is so great in less privileged social groups. Do economic difficulties make people long to hear the dramatic events of which they are deprived in the drudgery of daily life? To this might be added the fact that radio dramatizations, somewhat "written down" to a lower class audience, provide the main story material which is available to people in those social strata where reading has never become a matter of routine. Just what are the appeals which make those dramatic programs so successful with the lower income groups? Can the analysis of such appeals help us to anticipate some of the potentialities which radio would have as a tool of emotional propaganda?

Advertisers were eager to learn the income levels of listeners, and companies like CAB and C. E. Hooper obliged them with plenty of data. Listeners were ranked from "A" to "D," with "A" being the highest income group, estimated according to their home address. Reports were generally made in the form of tables and graphs.

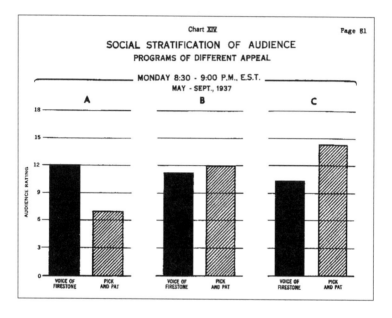

Chart entitled Social Stratification of Audience
Source: Beville, *op. cit.*, p. 81.

Tie-in ads for cigarettes featuring Dick Powell.

In the 1930s, stations not only worked to prove that they had listeners, they did everything they could think of to get new listeners. Their strategies included such tactics as making announcements on the air, getting radio shows or stars mentioned in newspaper stories, and putting posters on delivery trucks. In addition, tie-in ads and promotions were developed with program sponsors.

Radio's Golden Age

Radio's celebrated "Golden Age" began around 1925 and ended around 1950. Those who experienced it remember it with greater affection and nostalgia than people are liable to lavish on television any time in the future. Why did radio capture the hearts of the public so completely?

Perhaps it was because radio made itself a welcome visitor in the household. Families eagerly gathered around the radio console (then often a handsome piece of furniture) and listened together to news, music, drama, or comedy. Of course, families gather around the television today, but radio was different in one important respect. It didn't capture the gaze. It allowed family members to stay connected with each other, maintaining eye contact as they shared their reactions to whatever they listened to. If television has become notorious for dividing families, radio was beloved for drawing them together.

Another part of radio's great attraction during its Golden Age was its appeal to the imagination. Radio reached the listener by way of only one sense — the sense of hearing. This left plenty of room for the listener to visualize and dream.

Thus radio seemed to humanize whatever it brought into the home, making the world itself feel part of the intimate family circle. This was important during the first half of this century. The Golden Age of Radio included the Great Depression, World War II, and many other troubling and violent events and upheavals. It was a time that desperately needed humanizing.

The Hindenburg

Radio's eloquence in the face of great tragedy was well demonstrated on May 6, 1937. That was when journalist Herbert Morrison covered the arrival of the German Zeppelin Hindenburg *for Chicago station WLS.*

The Hindenburg *was the world's first transatlantic commercial airship, kept aloft by 7,000,000 cubic feet of hydrogen. In 1936, the* Hindenburg *began the first scheduled air service across the North Atlantic—a flight which took between fifty and sixty hours each way. It was truly a luxury ship, boasting a library, a dining room with lounge, and magnificent windowed corridors. The* Hindenburg *could carry more than seventy passengers, along with mail and cargo.*

Because the airship's arrival was no longer considered hot news, Morrison's words were recorded on discs rather than broadcast live. That day, thirty-six people died, most of them passengers. The following is a partial transcription of Morrison's moment-by-moment account of the Hindenburg *crash.*

Source: George N. Gordon and Irving A. Falk, *On-the-Spot Reporting: Radio Records History,* New York: Julian Messner, 1967. pp. 95-96.

She is practically standing still now. The ropes have been dropped and they have been taken hold of by a number of men on the field. It is starting to rain again. The rain has slacked up a bit. The back motors of the ship are holding her just enough to keep her from —

(The explosion occurred at this point!)

Get out of the way! Get this Charley! Get out of the way, please. *She's bursting into flames! This is terrible!* This is one of the worst catastrophes in the world. The flames are shooting five hundred feet up in the sky. It is a terrific crash, ladies and gentleman. It is in smoke and flames now. Oh, the humanity! Those passengers! I can't talk, ladies and gentlemen. Honest, it's a mass of smoking wreckage. Lady, I am sorry. Honestly, I can hardly—I am going to step inside where I can see it. Charley, that is terrible. Listen, folks, I am going to have to stop for a minute because I have lost my voice....

Morrison Describes His Experience

Many years later, in 1966, Morrison described what it was like to make broadcast history on that terrible day.

Source: Gordon and Falk, *op. cit.*, pp. 96-7. [All ellipses are in Gordon and Falk except for those after "searing brilliant drops of rain," which indicate a deletion on the part of the editor.]

As I talked, tears filled my eyes and I immediately thought "this can't be happening, I am telling a lie, what will my mother say..." but I kept talking and describing what was happening...the flames several hundred feet into the sky...and the molten metal dripping from the sky like searing brilliant drops of rain....One elderly lady standing beside me, apparently awaiting the arrival of a loved one, started to weave...I switched microphone to my right arm...and caught her as she swooned...but had to keep on talking. If you heard the complete description I gave, you will have heard me say to her, 'I'm sorry lady.' Someone realized the predicament I was in and came to my rescue and took her out of my arm. It all happened so fast, just a little over thirty seconds...from catching of fire...until the crash.

Broadcasting Sports

In addition to incidents like the Hindenburg *crash, radio brought other events to an enormous audience. In 1926, the Dempsey-Tunney title fight was heard around the world. That same year, the World Series baseball games were broadcast. In both cases, the next day's newspapers printed verbatim accounts from the radio broadcasts. Radio was big news, and sports continued to be big news on radio.*

On June 22, 1938, Joe Louis, the heavyweight boxing champion, met German fighter Max Schmeling in Yankee Stadium in New York. In 1936, Louis had lost a fight to Schmeling by a knockout and many people expected the same result again. Schmeling was a devout Nazi and had made ugly racist comments about the fact that Louis was an African-American. The fight lasted only two minutes and four seconds. Sports announcer Clem McCarthy described the match from the opening gong.

Source: George N. Gordon and Irving A. Falk, *On-the-Spot Reporting: Radio Records History*, New York: Julian Messner, 1967, pp. 102-104.

And there we are…They get into the ring right together with Arthur Donovan [the referee] stepping round them, and Joe Louis is in the center of the ring and Max is going around. Joe Louis lets hit with two straight lefts to the chin, both of them light, but as the men clinch Joe Louis tries to get over two hard lefts, and Max ties them up and breaks away clean.

On the far side of the ring, now, Max, with his back to the ropes and Louis hooks a left to Max's head quickly and shoots over a hard right to Max's head. Louis, a left to Max's jaw; a right to his head. Max shoots a hard right to Louis. Louis, with the old one-two: first the left and then the right! He's landed more blows in this one round than he landed in any five rounds of the other fight. And there Max Schmeling caught him with his guard down and crossed that right hand to Louis's paw, but Louis was going the way of the punch at the time. Now Max is backing away against the ropes, and Louis is following him and watching for that chance. He is crowding Schmeling. Schmeling is not stepping around very much, but his face is already marked. And they step into a fast clinch, and at close range Louis fights desperately to bring up a left to the jaw and a right to the body.

And coming out of that clinch he got over a hard right and stabbed Max with a good straight left jab. And Max backs away. And missed a right. Louis then tops him with two straight lefts to the face and brought over that hard right to the head, high on the temple. And Max tied him up in a clinch and broke 'round — his back against the ropes there — not too close on the ropes — Louis out, and Louis missed with a left swing but in close, brought up a hard right, a right to the jaw, and again a right to the body, a left hook, a right to the head, a left to the head, a right. Schmeling is going down!

But he held to his feet! Held to the ropes — looked to his corner in helplessness, and Schmeling is *down*! Schmeling is down! The count is four — it's — and he's up! And Louis — right and left to the head, a left to the jaw, a right to the head and the German is watching carefully. Louis measures him. Right to the body. A left hook to the jaw and *Schmeling is down*. The count is five-five-six-seven-eight….

The men are in the ring. The fight is over on a technical knockout! Max Schmeling is beaten in *one round*!…

Rumors of War

At the time of the Louis-Schmeling fight, the whole world seemed poised on the brink of a catastrophic war for the second time during the 20th century. Radio had not been ready to bring World War I into everyone's living rooms. But it was more than ready for World War II.

In March of 1938, Hitler annexed the nation of Austria to his German Reich. In September of that year, he turned toward Czechoslovakia. A conference was held in Munich Sept. 29-30, 1938, in which representatives from Britain and France consented to Hitler's demand for German occupation of parts of Czechoslovakia.

In New York City, H. V. Kaltenborn was responsible for the CBS coverage of the Munich crisis. He reported that Americans were staying glued to their radio sets as never before. Kaltenborn described the newsroom scene.

Source: Gordon and Falk, *op. cit.*, p. 111.

...News bulletins were handed to me as I talked. Speeches of foreign leaders had to be analyzed and sometimes translated while they were being delivered. In addition, split-second timing, always essential, became one of the physical requirements of network operation. I had to keep a constant eye on the control room for signs telling me when I was on or off the air. Sometimes when I had just launched into an analysis of some foreign leader's speech I was given a signal to wind up my talk in exactly one minute. This meant that I had to conclude my remarks in some sort of orderly and logical fashion as I watched the seconds tick away on the studio clock....

Broadcasting a War

In 1939, when Germany invaded Poland, Britain and France declared war on the Nazis. People's worst fears were realized; the world was at war again — although the United States wouldn't join the conflict until 1941. Broadcasters rushed to set up coverage of the war. News analyst Elmer David described the technical logistics of bringing war news into American homes.

Source: Elmer David, CBS News Analyst, "War News: Europe is Next Door Via Radio Coverage," in *The 1940 Radio Annual*, compiled by the staff of Radio Daily, Jack Alicoate, Editor, p. 47.

I was in the city room of the New York "Times" on August 1, 1914, and in the press room of CBS on September 1, 1939. This war is likely to differ in many respects from the one that went before, but one difference has been apparent from the outset. It was the first time the peoples of the world could hear a war actually breaking out.

An early transmission of a news broadcast by NBC (National Archives)

We heard the voice of Hitler announcing his "counter-attack" on Poland, the voice of Chamberlain admitting the collapse of "peace in our time." This is something so new that nobody yet realizes its possibilities. We at CBS have been working so close to it that all we can tell is just what happened....

Columbia's technical contribution — the four-way hookups between London, Paris, New York and Washington — had been worked out months before. Kaltenborn or I in New York talked with Ed Murrow in London, Tom Grandin in Paris and Albert Warner in Washington, just as if the four of us were seated around the same dinner table. The way it works is this: the conversations take place on only two transatlantic point-to-point short-wave channels, one eastbound to Europe, the other westbound to America. Land-lines carry the voices between New York and Washington, and between London and Paris. Thus each of the four cities is connected by a continuous loop of telephonic short-wave and land-line facilities. Each city is on a complete conversational basis.

From a London Rooftop

In 1939, Edward R. Murrow began broadcasting World War II reports from London. During air raids, when everyone else headed for shelter, Murrow often described the scene from a London rooftop. The following broadcast excerpt is from September 21.

Source: Gordon and Falk, *op. cit.*, pp. 28-29.

I'm standing on a roof top looking out over London ....For reasons of national as well as personal security, I'm unable to tell you the exact location from which I'm speaking. Off to my left, far away in the distance, I can see just that faint red, angry snap of anti-aircraft bursts against the steel blue sky, but the guns are so far away that it's impossible to hear them from this location. About five minutes ago, the guns were working...I think probably in a minute we shall have the sound of the guns in the immediate vicinity. The lights are swinging over in this general direction now. You'll hear two explosions. There they are! That was the explosion overhead, not the guns themselves. I should think in a few minutes there may be a hit of shrapnel around here. Coming in—moving a little closer all the while. The [German] plane's still very high. Earlier this evening we could hear occasional...again those were explosions overhead. Earlier this evening we heard a number of bombs go sliding and slithering across to fall several blocks away. Just overhead now the burst of anti-aircraft fire. Still the guns are not working. The searchlights now are feeling almost directly overhead. Now you'll hear two bursts a little nearer in a moment. ...There they are! That hard, stony sound.

A Soldier Reports

Broadcasters reported World War II from anywhere they could get near the action. A soldier-reporter broadcast from Kwajalein, a coral atoll in the Pacific:

Source: Gordon and Falk, *op. cit.*, p. 134.

The troops landed here about fifteen minutes ago. I don't know whether I sound scared or not, but I am. ...Lightning and just everything in the world is going off around this place...and, boy, this is really a hot place, and these charges keep coming over here, boy, and they come awfully close — awfully close. The Marines have landed. The situation is not in their hands as yet. However, we *have* hopes.

The Marines have started a full raid now....They're going in to a lot of fire, *but they're going in*, not stopping for anything. (Off mike: "Who?" — "Where?") Well, I'll be doggoned! Well, this island! You wouldn't believe that a thing would be living on it, and here is a *chicken*, just come over the hill right down in our shell hole, very nonchalantly pecking, scratching around in the sand, not singed a bit! That's good, isn't it? Of course, all the group of men who were moving around very cautiously forward are all getting a big laugh out of it. All the men!

Radio Storytelling

In dire times of depression and war, audiences often needed to be diverted from their problems. Radio attended to this need. Naturally, it brought comedy and music into people's homes. But it proved especially powerful when it came to telling stories. In the 1930s, the airwaves were filled with drama — crime fighters such as The Shadow, The Green Hornet, Dick Tracy, Jack Armstrong, Jungle Jim; cowboys such as the Lone Ranger and Tonto, Sergeant Preston and his "wonder dog" Yukon King; soap operas such as Ma Perkins, Helen Trent, and One Man's Family. All the narrative genres that we see on television today were first developed for radio. One of the great innovators in this field was director/writer/actor Orson Welles.

Welles was only sixteen when he starred on stage at the Abbey Theater in Dublin, Ireland. Returning home to Chicago, he helped to form a successful theater company and supplemented his earnings with appearances in radio dramas. In 1938, he directed a radio adaptation of H.G. Wells' The War of the Worlds. *The program went on the air Sunday evening, October 30. It was soon after the Munich crisis, and a nervous nation took the story all too seriously.*

Source: "The War of the Worlds," Mercury Theater on the Air, CBS, October 30, 1938, from Erik Barnouw, *The Golden Web: A History of Broadcasting in the United States*, Volume II-1933 to 1953, New York: Oxford University Press, 1968, pp. 86-87.

...It was near the end of October. Business was better. The war scare was over. More men were back at work. Sales were picking up. On this particular evening, October 30, the Crossley service estimated that thirty-two million people were listening to their radios.

> ANNOUNCER: For the next twenty-four hours not much change in temperature. A low pressure area over the northeastern states, bringing a forecast of rain, accompanied by winds of light gale force. Maximum temperature 66, minimum 48. This weather report comes to you from the Government Weather Bureau.
>
> We now take you to the Meridian Room in the Hotel Park Plaza in downtown New York, where you will be entertained by the music of Ramon Raquello and his orchestra.

The music that followed sounded just like what it was claimed to be. But it was soon interrupted.

> ANNOUNCER: Ladies and gentlemen, we interrupt our program of dance music to bring you a special bulletin from the Intercontinental Radio News. At twenty minutes before eight, Central Time, Professor Farrell of the Mount Jennings Observatory, Chicago, Illinois, reports observing several explosions of incandescent gas, occurring at regular intervals on the planet Mars. The spectroscope indicates the gas to be hydrogen and moving toward the earth with enormous velocity. Professor Pierson of the observatory at Princeton confirms Farrell's observation, and describes the phenomenon as

"like a jet of blue flame shot from a gun." We return you to the music of Ramon Raquello.

As the radio play continued in this fashion — announcing the landing of strange objects in New Jersey and other locations, describing ray-weapons that caused buildings, automobiles, and trees to burst into flame — panic began to break out across the country. People telephoned newspapers, police stations, and priests. Some tried to flee areas "under attack." In New York, sailors on shore leave were called back to their ships. Erik Barnouw comments, "The panic had one immediate effect on broadcast policy. Interruptions for fictional news bulletins became taboo in broadcast drama." (Barnouw, *op. cit.*, page 88.)

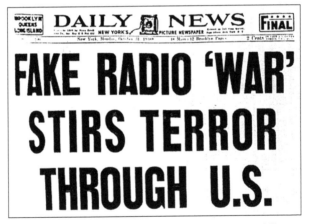

A sample of one of the many front page stories following the broadcast

Welles on Radio Drama

Orson Welles continued his role as an innovator in radio drama until he shifted his energies primarily to film making. In 1940 he expressed some of his thoughts on the nature of this new form of storytelling.

Source: Orson Welles, "Radio Drama: Progress of Drama in Broadcasting," *The 1940 Radio Annual*, compiled by the staff of *Radio Daily*, Jack Alicoate, Editor, p. 55.

Although radio has been with us for twenty years it must not be forgotten that in its function as a medium for projection of drama it is still in a highly experimental stage. It is only the gratifying successes of a few dramatic programs that gives us any assurance that we are finding valid methods for offering drama on the air. Radio, of course, is ideally suited for the transmission of news, the broadcasting of music and of comedy because by the mere act of reciting news into a microphone, of playing music or by telling jokes, the best form automatically is accomplished. Drama is another thing.

Drama

The less a radio drama resembles a play the better it is likely to be. This is not to indicate for one moment that radio drama is a lesser thing. It must be, however, drastically different. This is because the nature of the radio demands a form impossible to the stage. The images called up by a broadcast must be imagined, not seen. And so we find that radio drama is more akin to the form of the novel, to story telling, than to anything else of which it is convenient to think.

Certainly radio drama is the first new method of projecting entertainment which has come along since the invention of talkies and the animated cartoon. We are still in the midst of discovering valid techniques for its operation....The first person singular method of having the teller of the story also a character in it is now widely used by all first-class radio dramatists. To hear a voice saying "I am Hamlet" is dramatically more interesting than to hear a commentator say, "You are now going to hear from Hamlet."

Progress

Radio drama has done another thing. It has continued the process of bringing the actor near the audience, a development which has been detectible for about a hundred years. The actor's problem of projection has ceased to be troublesome and the test of a good performance has come to be its honesty and integrity....

Future

Looking ahead, I see radio as a great field for the presentation of literary and poetic images; as the coming great field for fantasy. The most important and interesting recent experiments in radio have been in these departments. Radio can do things which the realistic theater cannot and which, because of the multiplicity of images, would be impractical in the films. A few words can conjure up a scene beyond the furthest extension of the powers of the boldest and most resourceful technicians.

This is radio's strongest challenge to the existing mediums of entertainment. Is it commercial? Can you argue, in these days of "Snow White" and "Pinocchio" that radio fantasy cannot be as good box office as romance?

Program Codes for Stories on the Air

As radio gained power and influence, the controversy concerning what should be allowed on the air continued. By the end of the 1930s, intense criticism was coming in from some listeners about the amount of violence in programs heard by juveniles in radio drama. Both NBC and CBS established codes for programs in the mid-thirties, which they revised and reissued in the forties.

Source: NBC statement of policies in Variety, September 12, 1945, p. 30. (From J. Fred MacDonald, *Don't Touch that Dial! Radio Programming in American Life*, 1920-1960, Chicago: Nelson-Hall, 1979, p. 45.)

All stories must reflect respect for law and order, adult authority, good morals and clean living. The hero and heroine, and other sympathetic characters must be portrayed as intelligent and morally courageous. The theme must stress the importance of mutual respect of one man for another, and should emphasize the desirability of fair play and honorable behavior. Cowardice, malice, deceit, selfishness and disrespect for law must be avoided in the delineation of any character presented in the light of a hero to the child listener.

Source: CBS statement of policies in *Variety*, November 7, 1945, p. 40. (From MacDonald, *op. cit.*, page 45.)

The exalting, as modern heroes, of gangsters, criminals, and racketeers will not be allowed.

Disrespect for either parental or other proper authority must not be glorified or encouraged.

Cruelty, greed, and selfishness must not be presented as worthy motivations.

Programs that arouse harmful nervous reactions in the child must not be presented.

Conceit, smugness or unwarranted sense of superiority over others less fortunate may not be presented as laudable.

Recklessness and abandon must not be closely identified with a healthy spirit of adventure.

Unfair exploitation of others for personal gain must not be made appealing or attractive to the child.

Dishonesty and deceit are not to be made appealing or attractive to the child.

Racial Inequality on Radio

The Golden Age of Radio didn't offer equal opportunity for all. Roles for women and for various nationalities were usually stereotyped. For African-Americans, the situation was even worse. During the 1940s, America fought in a terrible war against the intolerance and bigotry of Hitler's Nazism. To some people, it seemed painfully ironic that intolerance and bigotry continued to exist on this side of the Atlantic — particularly on the nation's airwaves. In 1946, William H. Tymons, Secretary of the Washington Veterans Congress, offered this criticism of the portrayal of blacks on radio. His letter appeared in the trade newspaper Variety, *on March 27.*

[Radio depicts] the American Negro as a buffoon, lazy, shiftless, superstitious, ignorant, loose and servile. If the Negro menial is a good workman, he is again caricatured as ignorant, cunning and servile. If he has any schooling, he becomes in many instances even more the target for the vicious, evil stupidity of our hatemongers. It goes without saying that this "typing" of the entire race is false and distorted. This is not the democratic way of life for which so many of our fallen comrades paid so dearly with their lives. This is the Hitler pattern. This is American fascism.

A Plea for Understanding and Toleration

To many white celebrities who contributed their talents and energies to the war effort, it seemed only patriotic to resist bigotry at home. Some publicly declared their own sympathy and solidarity with African-Americans. In 1945, Kate Smith, one of radio's most influential personalities, made the following speech on the program We the People.

Source: A speech by Kate Smith, published in *Tune In*, May, 1945, p. 22. (From MacDonald, *op. cit.*, p. 354.)

Well, I'm not an expert on foreign affairs — and I don't pretend to know all the complex things that will have to be done for a lasting peace. But I am a human being — and I do know something about people. I know that our statesmen — our armies of occupation — our military strategists — may all fail if the peoples of the world don't learn to understand and tolerate each other. Race hatreds — social prejudices — religious bigotry — they are the diseases that eat away all the fibres of peace....And where are they going to be exterminated? At a conference table in Geneva? Not by a long shot. In your own city — your church — your children's school — perhaps in your own home. You and I must do it — every father and mother in the world, every teacher, everyone who can rightfully call himself a human being.

A New Code

In 1951, after a series of meetings with representatives of the NAACP and the National Urban League, NBC released a new code concerning program content.

Source: *Variety*, July 18, 1951, page 1. (From MacDonald, *op. cit.*, page 364.)

All program materials present with dignity and objectivity the varying aspects of race, creed, color, and national origin. The history, institutions and citizens of all nations are fairly represented....Defamatory statements or derogatory references expressed or implied, toward an individual, nationality, race, group, trade, profession, industry, or institution are not permitted.

Epilogue

To speak of radio's "Golden Age" is perhaps slightly misleading. It implies that radio has been in a decline since around 1950. True, it was then that television took hold of the public's fancy and radio listenership dropped off sharply. Perhaps most sadly, the unique art of radio storytelling has almost vanished.

But radio found a different niche after the advent of television, focusing on news, music, and talk shows. If radio does not command the American living room like it used to, it certainly dominates the workplace, the automobile, and other parts of the house. While it is a rare household that doesn't own at least one television, it is a rarer household that doesn't own several radios.

Most importantly, we still find reasons to listen to our radios. Radio has proved particularly valuable in times of crisis and natural disaster; a battery-powered radio can supply essential information to a community when television service is knocked out. Radio still continues to generate its own unique celebrities. It also maintains its power to arouse controversy and anxiety, particularly with the growth of call-in talk shows. Although it may seem less visible than during its Golden Age, radio is as much a part of our lives as ever.